R. Curtis

The Sabbath

A concise Bible history of the Israelitish or Jewish Sabbaths

R. Curtis

The Sabbath
A concise Bible history of the Israelitish or Jewish Sabbaths

ISBN/EAN: 9783337102319

Printed in Europe, USA, Canada, Australia, Japan

Cover: Foto ©Lupo / pixelio.de

More available books at **www.hansebooks.com**

THE SABBATH.

—— A CONCISE ——

Bible History of the Israelitish or Jewish

——

SABBATHS,

EMBRACING THE SEVENTH DAY SABBATH,

—— AND ——

THE SEVEN YEARLY SABBATHS;

THEIR ORIGIN, USE AND END.

ALSO, THE ORIGIN, USE AND PERPETUITY

—— OF THE ——

CHRISTIAN SABBATH.

BY MR. R. CURTIS.

OTSEGO, MICHIGAN.

RECORD PRINTING CO., NEWS, BOOK & JOB PRINTERS.

1869.

THE SABBATH,

—— A CONCISE ——

BIBLE HISTORY OF THE ISRAELITISH

OR JEWISH

SABBATHS,

EMBRACING THE SEVENTH DAY SABBATH,

—— AND ——

THE SEVEN YEARLY SABBATHS;

THEIR ORIGIN, USE AND END.

ALSO, THE ORIGIN, USE AND PERPETUITY

—— OF THE ——

CHRISTIAN SABBATH.

BY MR. R. CURTIS

OTSEGO, MICHIGAN:

RECORD PRINTING COMPANY.

1869.

PREFACE.

THE prevalent diversity of opinions, respecting the Sabbath and its observance, suggested the following work, which is offered to the public, with the hope of harmonizing all the conflicting Sabbath views, on the basis of the Scriptures.

Within the last quarter of a century, a new church organization arose attracting much attention by their earnest advocacy of the seventh day of the week, as the proper and only day to be observed as the Sabbath day, "holy to our Lord." Very soon they asked and obtained legislative authority to work and carry on their occupations on the first day of the week, which had been, time out of mind, held to be the Christian Sabbath by nearly every Christian people in this and other countries. The Seventh-day Sabbath views, were opposed by various arguments, setting forth, that the Sabbath was changed from the seventh day, to the first day.

Unfortunately, however, for the truth, both contending parties were agreed in maintaining the error that originated the misunderstanding. Each party claiming the seventh day of creation as the origin of the Sabbath, with four thousand years of unabated obligation upon all mankind, made the institution of universal application. Upon this unauthorized assumption of origin, its long standing would indicate that the Seventh day was of perpetual obligation; giving to the Seventh day view, the greater weight of argument.

CHAPTER I.

ORIGIN OF THE SABBATH.

"SABBATH is holy rest unto the Lord; to-morrow is the rest of the holy Sabbath unto the Lord;" Exodus 16—23. See also, 25th verse. " To-day is a Sabbath unto the Lord. This day is holy unto the Lord your God;" Nehemiah 8—9. It is not therefore a rest from weariness, or a physical rest; that being always a proper subject of human legislation, but holy rest never. The days appointed to celebrate and keep holy rest unto the Lord, are called Sabbath days, holy days, and holy convocations. These terms are synonymous, as used in Scripture. " Six days shall work be done, but the seventh day is the Sabbath of rest, an holy convocation; " Leviticus 23—3. See also verses 32 and 39; compare Numbers 29—7, and 12th. Sabbath days were the appointed means, chosen of God, to supplant and destroy idol worship, which had become universal at the time of the calling of Abraham. Through its long established practice, the people had ceased to know the true God, and were ascribing to idols the authorship and work of creation. The Sabbath days were eight in number; seven that occurred once a year, and the weekly or seventh day Sabbath. They were the result of a series of miracles, signs and wonders, of a nature and character to disprove idolatry, and manifest and set forth the true God. Miracles were the evidence or testimony that God gave of himself; and were a necessity of those ages and people, arising from their belief in, and acceptance of idolatry as the true worship. The miracles in their nature, character and extent, furnished all nations a full and complete foundation on which to predicate an intelligent belief in the true God, and consequent disbelief in idols. The Sabbath days were memorial days, which gathered together and celebrated in divine services, all the mighty miracles, signs

and wonders wrought from the calling of Abraham, to the restoration of Israel from the hand of Pharaoh, King of Egypt.
The Sabbath days were appointed and set apart to celebrate
and keep in memory, the testimony and evidence of the divine
existance, manifested and made known through miracles, and
were rendered *holy* by their exclusion from all survile labor
and work. Moreover, Sabbath, or holy rest unto the Lord,
was constituted a *covenant* on Mount Sinai; Exodus 31—16.
Wherefore the children of Israel shall keep the Sabbath, to
observe the Sabbath throughout their generations for a perpetual covenant; verse 17. It is a sign between me and the
children of Israel forever.

The whole constellation of Sabbath days of holy rest unto
the Lord, which included the seventh-day Sabbath, and the
seven annual Sabbath days, was constituted a covenant sign, to
be kept and observed by Israel, throughout their generations.
The Sabbath days in divine forms of worship, was a public
profession before all the heathen, that the Lord which " made
heaven and earth, the sea and all that in them is," was their
God; "therefore ye are my witnesses, that I am God:" Isaiah
43—12. This covenent sign of Sabbath days distinguished
Israel from all the heathen, whose sign everywhere was idolatry and its worship.

For the important reason that the eight Sabbath days were
one, or as one day in the covenant, therefore the frequent occurrence of the weekly and the yearly Sabbaths upon the same
day, was a celebration of harmonious events, avoiding confu-
sion in object and worship.

The object of all this divine testimony of miracles, signs
and wonders, gathered up and celebrated in Sabbath days, was
to make his name known throughout all the earth; " That my
name may be declared_throughout all the earth," Exodus, 9—
16. It was divine Providence using means to call the idolatrous world back to himself; therefore the divine name was
declared throughout all the earth, in the keeping and observance of his Sabbath covenant sign, by making Israel a fear and
a terror to all the heathen nations. " This day will I begin to

put the dread of thee and the fear of thee upon the nations that are under the whole Heaven," Deuteronomy, 2—25. And all people of the earth shall see that thou art called by the name of the Lord, and they shall be afraid of thee; chapter 28—10.

Sabbath observance, therefore, was Israel's protection and safety against all nations. "Neither shall any man desire thy land, when thou shalt go up to appear before the Lord thy God, thrice in the year." Exodus, 34—24.

The assembling together of all Israel from remote and distant parts of their country, so frequently, and for such a length of time, would, in the nature of the case, afford the heathen an opportunity to over run their country and dispossess them of their land; but the observance of the Sabbath covenant sign that called Israel together thrice in the year, instructed the heathen as well as Israel, of the invisible presence that smote the first born, that divided the sea before them, that, spoiled Egypt for Israel's sake had the salutary effect to remove the desire of the heathen to enter upon Israel's unprotected lands, while they were gone up to worship on the Sabbath days.

Sabbath covenant keeping, therefore, invested Israel with perfect security and safety. Without this provision of protection in the covenant, Israel, among the nations, would have been as a lamb among wolves. The original miracles—smiting the first born, the overthrow of Pharaoh and the dividing of the sea—were reproduced in the memorial observance, putting the heathen in fear, while Israel, as a consequence of that fear and terror, enjoyed security and safety. Also in breaking and forsaking this covenant sign, holy rest unto the Lord, the divine purpose was not frustrated; His name was declared in breaking the covenant as in keeping it. Even all nations shall say, wherefore hath the Lord done thus unto this Land? "What meaneth the heat of this great anger?" Then men shall say, "because they have forsaken the covenant of the Lord God of their fathers which he made with them when he brought them forth out of the land of Egypt, for they went and served other Gods." Deuteronomy, 29, 22 to 28. The first covenant, see

Hebrews 5—7. was composed of two parts: first, the covenant
made with Abraham: second, the covenant made with Israel
on Mount Sinai. The latter covenant was a supplement added
to the former, because of transgressions: the transgressions
complained of being idolatry. Israel in bondage to Egypt,
had become worshipers of idols. See Ezekiel, 20, 7 and 8.
"Then said I unto them, cast ye away every man, the abomina-
tions of his eyes, and defile not yourselves with the idols of
Egypt." See verse 5 to 20.

The divine purpose in calling Abraham, was to make of
him a new nation, whose God was the Lord: therefore he
would not drive out of Canaan the idolatrous Amorite and
bring in the seed of Abraham and plant them a nation of idol-
aters. The Mount Sinai covenant of Sabbath days was added
to abolish this idolatry, and was means adapted to that end.
It was the counterpart added to make the covenant of promise
to Abraham available. "Cursed be the man that obeyeth not
the words of this covenant which I commanded your fathers
in the day that I brought them forth out of the land of Egypt,
from the iron furnace, saying, obey my voice, and do them according to all which I command you: so shall ye be my people
and I will be your God: That I may perform the oath which I
have sworn unto your fathers, to give them a land flowing with
milk and honey, as it is this day." Jeremiah 11th, 3 to 5. The
Mount Sinai covenant of Sabbath-days of holy rest unto the
Lord, enforced by the death penalty in the wilderness, was the
divinely appointed means, going before and preparing the way
for the performance of the oath. "That I may perform the
oath which I have sworn unto your fathers." The Mount Sinai
covenant of Sabbath days, the Sabbath law, written on tables
of stone, table of the covenant, tables of testimony, gathered
the testimony of the true God into Sabbath days "And remember that thou wast a servant in the land of Egypt, and
that the Lord thy God brought thee out thence through a
mighty hand, and by a stretched out arm: therefore the Lord
thy God commanded thee to keep the Sabbath day." Deuteronomy 5—15.

Prior to the Mount Sinai covenant, the testimony of the true God, without Sabbath days, was made known to Abraham, Isaac and Jacob, in a daily personal experience of that divine providence and protection, that reproved kings, that suffered no man to do them wrong when they went from one nation to another, from one kingdom to another people. Psa. 105. The testimony of the true God without Sabbath days, that kept the fathers Abraham, Isaac and Jacob from idolatry under great exposure among the heathen, was joined to "the testimony of Israel," in the songs of the sanctuary on the Sabbath days, constituting the nation's history of divinely ordered events, a history of miracles, a store-house of wisdom and knowledge, gathered up by the inspired psalmist, clothed with inspired language, from age to age made available to all Israel in Sabbath worship. Throughout the generations of Israel, the nation's history of past ages of divine providence and mighty miracles, was recalled by Sabbath memorial, Exodus 12—14, brought back in Sabbath celebrations, Leviticus 23d, 32 to 41, and repeated in psalms and divine songs on stringed instruments in the sanctuary on the Sabbath days. The nation's history poured forth in the songs of the sanctuary, was the people's book, and served instead of the printed page. This was the order of divine economy "till the seed should come to whom the promise was made."

CHAPTER II.

SABBATH COMMANDMENT: WHERE FOUND.

The conflicting views upon Sabbath observance, originates in a misapprehension of the Sabbath commandment.

Eighth to eleventh verse, of the 20th chapter of Exodus, has been universally accepted as the Sabbath commandment, "written and engraven in stones." This error has been productive of conflicting views and practice.

The 20th chapter of Exodus was written in the book of

the Law, more than forty days prior to giving the first tables
of stone; and contains only an epitome of the Sabbath commandment. After the 20th chapter of Exodus was written in
the book of the Law and read in the audience of the people,
Exodus 24th chapter, Moses was called up into the Mount,
where he tarried forty days: at the end of which time, he received the first tables of stone.

These being broken, he went up the second time, Exodus
34—1, remaining forty days, at which time he received the
second tables of stone, with a commandment to write the
words therein contained: "Write thou these words," Exodus
34—27. This obligation enjoined upon Moses in the Mount,
is found fulfilled only at the fifth chapter of Deuteronomy, see
22d verse. Therefore the Sabbath commandment is found
only in Deuteronomy, fifth chapter, twelfth to fifteenth verse,
copied out of the tables of stone according to the commandment, "Write thou these words." This must be accepted as
the only verbatim copy of the Sabbath commandment on
record; as the book of the Law never contained but one copy
of that commandment written in tables of stone.

It will not be contended that two widely different Scriptures are both a verbatim copy of the Sabbath commandment,
written on tables of stone; This is too preposterous for belief.
A comparison of the two Scriptures, Exodus 20th chapter,
eighth to eleventh verse, with Deuteronomy 5th chapter 12th
to 15th verse, demonstrates that only one of the above named
Scriptures could have been copied out of the tables of stone.
In the absence of any and all adverse testimony, the twenty-
second verse of Deuteronomy 5th chapter, establishes the
point at issue.

It is evident from the 24th chapter of Exodus, that the
20th chapter was written from hearing of the ear, and from
memory of what was spoken in the Mount at different times,
and does not contain a verbatim copy of the ten commandments that was afterwards written in the tables of stone and
delivered to Moses on the Mount, with the commandment
"write thou these words." Exodus 34—27. The ten com-

mandments as they stand in the 20th chapter of Exodus, omit the testimony of the restoration of Israel from Egypt, commanded on tables of stone to be kept in Sabbath days, the keeping of which was keeping the covenant that he made with them in the day that he took them by the hand to bring them out of Egypt. To omit the testimony of divine interposition and providence in Egypt, would be to omit the Sabbath covenant altogether. This was sometimes done by Israel, in violation of the commandment; always resulting in the greatest calamity to the nation. Somebody blundered in supposing that Exodus 20th chapter, contained the ten commandments, and others have followed in their steps, without a proper consideration of the subject. The unanimous testimony of Scripture goes directly to prove that Deuteronomy, 5th chapter, contains the only verbatim copy of the ten commandments on record.

Therefore, to the fourth commandment, Sabbath law, written on tables of stone, Deuteronomy, 5—15, are unmistakably affixed its date, origin and nature, with circumstances of country and nations. The Sabbath commandment is founded in a demonstration of invisible divine power, put forth in sight of the heathen, Ezekiel 20th chapter, which break the bands of the nation of Egypt, and made the servant Israel to go out free. The nature of the Sabbath was a memorial of its origin and circumstances, as set forth in the commandment. "And remember that thou wast a servant in the land of Egypt, and that the Lord thy God brought thee out thence through a mighty hand, and by a stretched out arm; therefore the Lord thy God commanded thee to keep the Sabbath day."

The commandment renders impossible any truth in the theory that the Sabbath was appointed at the Creation, two thousand years antecedent to the existence of the nations of Egypt and Israel and the occurrence of the events on which the Sabbath is founded. The prevalent theory that the seventh day of Creation was a Sabbath and every seventh day thereafter, is based on Genesis 2—2 and 3, and Exodus 20—11, neither of which scriptures afford any proof that the seventh day of creation was appointed a holy Sabbath day; to which, also, it may further be replied:

First, Sabbath obligations were accompanied by promises of blessings in obedience, and penalties in disobedience, which took place in accordance with the facts, and with as much publicity.

Second, Sabbath was appointed to subvert idol worship, which did not exist at the creation, and is not known to have existed prior to the deluge.

Third, If a Sabbath was in force during the first period of two thousand years of the world's history, there would have been some trace of its benefits upon those who observed it, or harm following its desecration and neglect; and the people in after ages, upon whom a Sabbath was made obligatory, had a right to the benefit of such facts, and their importance was too great to be passed by or overlooked by the divine historian. It is not possible that all the results, moral and physical, arising from Sabbath keeping or Sabbath desecration, for a period of two thousand and five hundred years, could be locked up in profound secrecy, beyond the ken of prophet or seer; no evidence of a Sabbath being found in the divine record during the first two thousand and five hundred years of sacred history. Beyond the usual occupations of men, the only known use of the seventh day of creation was in counting time by the cycle of seven days, which has been in use among all nations.

The advocates of a creational Sabbath, claim that Cain, Abel and Noah, were observers of a weekly Sabbath in their time. On which it may be observed that the words, *process of time*, Genesis 4—3, relied upon to prove *a weekly* offering, when applied to a tiller of the ground, bear no proper relation to a weekly period, but does well apply to the in-gathering of harvest, or offering of first fruits unto the Lord: for example, see Leviticus 23—10th and 14th verses, by which we are led to conclude that the offerings of Cain and Abel brought, *in process of time*, of the fruits of their occupations, was a yearly, and not a weekly offering.

Noah was favorably situated in the ark, to keep a Sabbath if a Sabbath was then in force: but we find him on the seventh day, experimenting with a raven and a dove, "to see if the waters were abated;" "doing his own ways, finding his own pleasure;" see Isaiah 58—13; continuing his work of observation upon the seventh day, until a satisfactory result was attained. "So Noah knew that the waters were abated." Genesis 8—7 to 12. "Where no law is, there is no transgression;" but this transaction would have incurred the death penalty under the Sabbath law, in the wilderness. Whosoever doeth any work in the Sabbath day he shall surely be put to death;" Exodus 31—15. Neither Cain, Abel or Noah, furnish any proof of a weekly Sabbath or holy day in their time.

The historical account of creation, comprising six days work and seventh day of rest. Exodus 20—11, has very generally been accepted as a part of the Sabbath law, written upon the tables of stone, proving, as is claimed, that the seventh day of creation was a Sabbath day. This error arises from misunderstanding the object of the transactions then taking place, which was not to declare the seventh day of creation a Sabbath day, but to undeceive the idolatrous heathen nations respecting the *origin* of the world and all things therein, and to confirm Israel in the truth of what Moses had taught them. See Exodus 19—9, and chapter 20—20; also Deuteronomy 5—23 to 27. The heathen believed that their idol gods made the world and all things therein; "mine idol, and my graven image, and my molten image hath commanded them;" Isaiah 48—5. To correct this world wide error, was the object of the historical account of creation. "For in six days the *Lord* made heaven and earth the sea and all that in them is, and rested the seventh day.

The object was to undeceive all the heathen as to the origin of all created things in heaven and in earth, looking first to reclaiming Israel from the belief and practice of idolatry, and also all other nations through them. "For it is a terrible thing that I will do with you."

The account of creation, Exodus 20—11, was written in the book of the law but not in the tables of stone; it is not a part of the covenant made with Israel on Mount Horeb. Deuteronomy 5—2 and 3. Exodus 20—11 is history and not commandments.

"Wherefore the Lord blessed the Sabbath day and hallowed it." Exodus 20—11. Not the seventh day and hallowed it. Sabbath is not a day, but holy rest unto the Lord; its existance depended upon ceasing from all *survile* labors. Therefore a divine example of ceasing from work on the seventh day is presented. "He also hath ceased from his own works as God did from his." Hebrews 4—10. "And he rested on the seventh day from all his work." Genesis 2—2. After six days of work, next in divine order is rest. Without observing this division of work and rest. Sabbath has no existence. and consequently no blessing. Let it be observed that Sabbath is not *the* day, nor *a* day. nor *any* day; the day is but the husk that protects the valued fruit. The appointed *day* is the time to engage in the duty, to keep and do the commandment. Sabbath is not a day, but a condition pertaining to holy, spiritual worship. ordered in all things and sure. It is over the duty and not over the day. that the worshipers have control.

The day returns in its appointed season. without regard to holy rest or profane use.

The correctness of this position is proven by Israel's seventy years captivity. caused by profaning with survile labors the appointed time for holy rest. See Nehemiah 13—15 to 18.

All the idolatrous heathen nations. from time immemorial had the seventh day, but none of them had the Sabbath; "they kept not the rest of the holy Sabbath unto the Lord," nor called it a delight. nor confessed its divine author. "They worshiped idols. the work of their own hands and mocked at Israel's Sabbaths." Lamentations 1 — 7. and consequently at Israel's God which brought them out of Egypt; "thou shalt have none other." See first commandment. Deuteronomy 5—6 to 7.

CHAPTER III.

THE YEARLY SABBATHS.

The annual or yearly Sabbaths were seven in number. Two in connection with the feast of the passover, two in connection with the feast of tabernacles, the Sabbath of trumpets, the Sabbath of atonement and the Sabbath of weeks. The passover and the feast of tabernacles were each a service of seven days; both opened and closed with a Sabbath or holy day. The yearly Sabbaths commemorated particular events and circumstances of divine testimony that required a more extended commemoration than was given in the weekly Sabbath service.

The passover commemorated the smiting of the first-born of Egypt, and the going out of the Children of Israel out of Egypt with a mighty hand. The feast of tabernacles commemorated the dwelling in booths by the sea, their passage through the sea and the overthrow of Pharaoh and his host in the mighty waters. This appears from the consideration that they had no other dwelling in booths in their passage out of Egypt. They having marched day and night (Exodus 13—21) until they came to the sea (chapter 14—9.) Their campings prior to reaching the Red Sea were for needful refreshments. "That your generations may know that I made the Children of Israel to dwell in booths when I brought them out of the land of Egypt." Leviticus 23—43. Nehemiah 8—15.

SABBATH OF TRUMPETS.

" In the seventh month, in the first day of the month, shall ye have a Sabbath, a memorial of blowing of trumpets, an holy convocation." Leviticus 23—24. The use of trumpets (See Numbers 10—9, Judges 7—20 to 22, Second Chronicles 13—12 to 14) in carrying consternation and fear to the hearts of the enemy, as it did to Israel in the day of the assembly beneath the Mount Sinai, (see Hebrews 12—18 to 21) would justify and warrant the belief that this service was a memorial of the long and loud sound of the trumpet on Mount Sinai. Exodus 19—16 to 19, and chapter 20—18.

SABBATH OF ATONEMENT

"Also, on the tenth day of this seventh month, there shall be a day of atonement: it shall be an holy convocation unto you, and ye shall afflict your souls." Leviticus 23—27 to 32. This Sabbath service doubtless cemmemorated the many and great afflictions that Israel endured in Egypt, and may have more particular reference to that miraculous intervention of divine providence, causing opposite results to follow the systematic afflictions laid upon Israel to diminish them, by adding excessive rigor and cruelty to the ordinary hardships of a life of bondage. "And they made their lives bitter." "But the more they afflicted them the more they multiplied and grew. Exodus 1—10 to 15.

SABBATH OF WEEKS.

"When ye come into the land which I give unto you and shall reap the harvest thereof, then ye shall bring a sheaf of the first fruits of your havest." See Leviticus 23—10 to 21. "Also in the day of the first fruits when ye bring a new meat offering unto the Lord, after your weeks be out, ye shall have a holy convocation; ye shall do no survile work." Numbers 28—26. "And thou shalt remember that thou wast a bondman in Egypt, and thou shalt observe and do these statutes. See Deuteronomy 16—9 to 12.

This Sabbath service contrasted to great advantage, their condition in the land of Canaan, which was the glory of all lands, with their former condition of bondmen in Egypt.

CHAPTER IV.

"For if that first covenant had been faultless, then should no place have been sought for the second." Hebrews 8—7. A grouping together of national ordinances of divine service, was that first covenant; circumcision, Sabbath days, priest-hood, sacrifices and offerings for sin "Ordinances of divine service." *At that time* the only door by which the people of other nations could obtain recognition as the servants or people of God, (Isaiah 56—1 to 8,) was at *fault* with the new covenant, which is Christ, through whom all nations and people "have access by one spirit unto the Father." "For these are the two covenants, the one from Mount Sinai which gendereth to bondage, which is Agar." The Mount Sinai covenant which gendereth to bondage, had its birth in Egypt, at the institution of the passover, to which time, place and condition the Sabbath commandment pointed the Jewish worshipper to his former condition of bondman, as was that of Hagar and her son, and answers to Jerusalem and the Jew which now is, who desires to keep the testimony of that first covenant, of circumcision, Sab-bath days, priest-hood, sacrifices and offerings offered by the law, and is in spiritual bondage with her children. But the new covenant, "Jerusalem which is above, is free, which is the mother of us all." The two covenants are here represented by Hagar and Sarah, the bond and free women and their sons. "But as then, he that was born after the flesh, persecuted him that was born after the spirit, even so it is now. Nevertheless what sayeth the Scripture, "cast out the bondwoman and her son; for the son of the bondwoman shall not be heir with the son of the free woman."—See Galatians 4—21 to 30. This allegory represents the Mount Sinai covenant of Sabbath days, priest-hood and ordinances gendered or born in bondage, as cast out, as was Hagar and her son, having no part with the new covenant, represented by the free woman, which, however, the uninstructed Jewish converts desired to retain and follow. See verses 10 and 21. See also Acts 15—1 and 24.

A change of covenant was manifestly a foreordained event, when Moses came down from the Mount with the tables of the covenant in his hand. For which cause he "put a vail over his face that the Children of Israel could not steadfastly look to the end of that which is abolished." Second Corinthians Chapter 3. The vail was used to conceal from Israel the manifest destiny of that first covenant, "written and engraven in stones," which was to be done away; verse 7. Which is abolished; verse 13. The truth hidden from Israel beneath the vail, related to the temporary character of that first covenant which Moses brought down from the Mount; "which vail is done away in Christ."

At the first interview with the disciples after his resurrection, Christ expounded the things concealed by the vail, hidden in himself, beginning at Moses and all the prophets; Christ moved Moses and all the prophets to speak, therefore he is able to expound the word spoken, by which the disciples understood that the first covenant of circumcision, Sabbath days, priesthood, sacrifices and offerings for sin, had served out their appointed time, were thenceforth to have no force; to be as though they had not been.

It is believed by some that the seventh day Sabbath was exempt from the results and consequences of a change of covenant, and therefore remains of the same force and obligation as under the first covenant. This view is not supported by the scriptures.

First, its law of commandment, "written and engraven in stones," gave character to the tables of the covenant, as preeminently tables of testimony; testimony made and set forth in the country of Egypt, Israel and the Egyptians, actors in the scene, the nations beholding the things that were done. The seventh day Sabbath was essentially the same as the passover Sabbaths; covered the same ground. Their limited nature, understood by Moses, was concealed from Israel by the vail put over the face of Moses, expounded by Christ to the disciples, governing their action in abandoning the sabbath days and adopting the Lord's day in coming together to keep the testimony of Jesus, after his resurrection. See Acts 20—7.

Second, the seventh day Sabbath was inseparably one with the family of Sabbath days in sacrifices and offerings for sin, and was changed by the general law of limitation that changed all the sabbath days. "Made of necessity" by that inherent law of limitation that changed the priesthood, (Hebrews 7—12,) leaving no authorized priest to officiate or offer the Sabbath offerings.

Third, throughout the generations of Israel the Sabbath days in their proper observance, were days of gladness to Israel (Numbers 10—10) and days of fear and terror to the heathen nations, Deuteronomy 11—25,) hence the value of the covenant to Israel.

When all nations and people were to join in one memorial of the true God in Christ, this separating wall of Sabbath days was taken out of the way, nailed to his cross, and the Lord's day, without the associations of fear or hate or national prestige, was chosen for all men to join in one spirit and one memorial to keep the testimony of Jesus.

Fourth, the first covenant of sabbath days "written and engraven in stones" was rejected from the new covenant memorial, when the new covenant was promised; Jeremiah 31 —31 to 34. "Not according to the covenant that I made with their fathers in the day that I took them by the hand to bring them out of the land of Egypt." Which new covenant is explained in Second Corinthians 3—3; "written" not in tables of stone, but in fleshly tables of the heart. Therefore to put the seventh day "written and engraven in stones," in the place of t e Lord's day written in the fleshly tables of the heart, is to subvert the divine order and ministration.

Fifth, the limited character of the first covenant of sabbath days is made to appear beforehand, by Christ withholding the Sabbath commandment from the young man, the future of whose life was to be spent under new covenant obligations. See Matthew 19—17 to 20.

A formal change of covenant was instituted by Christ at the last passover, (See Luke 22—1 to 20,) by concentrating the divine testimony of both the old and new covenants in one memorial which is Christ, the body or substance, distinguished from the passing shadow of ordinances, by the new covenant memorial service; "this do in remembrance of me." "Having spoiled principalities and powers, (Colossians 2— 15, 16 and 17) having spoiled Egypt and the nations that stood in the way of the oath of promise to Abraham," he "made a shew of them, openly triumphing over them in it. Let no man, therefore, judge you in meat or drink or in respect of any holy day, which are a shadow of things to come, but the body is of Christ." These divinely appointed services, meat offerings, drink offerings and Sabbath days of the first covenant, stood in the place of Christ, the "one offering;" they were the shadow, waiting to vanish away. Christ having spoiled principalities and powers, appointed these services to keep the testimony of the true God in their spoilation, to shadow forth his divine glory till the fullness of time should come when these ordinances, meat offerings and drink offerings and holy days signifying national triumphs, should give place to the one offering of Christ; one memorial, one Lord's day for all men to observe the memorial and keep the testimony of Jesus, to keep and do the commandment. "This do in remembrance of me." See Luke 22—19.

CHAPTER V.

ORIGIN OF THE CHRISTIAN SABBATH.

The rebellious Israelites who came out of Egypt by Moses, (See Hebrews 3d and 4th chapters,) whose carcases fell in the wilderness, refused to walk in his law, to keep the rest of the holy Sabbath unto the Lord, not perceiving that they were services preparatory to entering and remaining in the promised land, Jeremiah 11—3 to 5, and Deuteronomy 28—64. In ordinances they did not see Jesus their Savior in the spoilation of principalities and powers, and therefore did not come to him in the use of those ordinances, and obtain the rest of spiritual worshipers, but indulged in rebellion, hardness of heart and unbelief, called uncircumcision of heart, in opposition to the commandment, by which the great benefits of a holy rest was lost to them. "Wherefore I was grieved with that generation and said they do always err." The error sought here to be corrected, was the belief that holy rest was abolished with the first covenant, with "the hand writing of ordinances that was against us." The apostle assures the christian converts that holy rest *remains* to the people of God, Hebrews 4—9, and also that its misuse will bring the same disastrous state of mind; "Lest any of you be hardened through the deceitfulness of sin;" "Lest any man fall after the same example of unbelief." "For if Jesus had given them rest," Hebrews 4—8,—rest of Jesus or rest to the soul was attainable by the church in the wilderness, in the use of means as at any other period of the church of Christ—"Then would he not *afterward* have spoken of another day." The contingency mentioned in the 8th verse not being realized, "again he limiteth a certain day," verse 7, not a day of survile labors, but of holy rest.

Again he limiteth a certain day saying in David, Hebrews 4—7. The day limited in David is not the seventh day of the Jewish week with unlimited memorial celebrating an unlimited number of mighty miracles covering the ground of all the

Sabbath days which gendereth to bondage; it is another day
spoken of *afterward*.—Hebrews 4—8.   Not the seventh day
Sabbath with its commandment written in tables of stone,
which would be the same day and not another.   The testimony
and ministration of another day spoken of, afterward was written, *not* in tables of stone, but in fleshy tables of the heart.
—Second Corinthians 3—3.   The day limited in David is re-
strained from a general signification of the great and sore
judgements upon Egypt. upon Pharaoh and his house, as seen
in Deuteronomy 6—20 to 22.   This testimony of the true God
was unlimited in its numerous memorial scenes as appears from
the book of Psalms, see Psalms 105 and 106, see also Acts 7—
36; but in Christ. the root and spring of David, Revealations
22—16.   The testimony of the true God, is limited to the resurrection of Christ from the dead.   " Whereof he hath given
assurance unto all men, in that he hath raised him from the
dead;" Acts 17—31.   Limited to the Lord's day by the res
urrection.   The first day of the week was made the Lord's
day by the resurrection; limited to one memorial, which is
Christ, as distinguished from the plurality of holy days and
memorials of the first covenant.   The resurrection day is
known to be that *certain* day spoken of afterward, *certain*,
assured in mind, not to be doubted; assured "unto all men."
The resurrection of Jesus on the first day of the week, opened
the new covenant with the Christians' holy rest, as the passover
opened the first covenant with a Jewish holy rest.   That was
testimony established on spoiling of principalities and powers.
—Colossians 2—15.   This on the spoiling of the powers of
death and the grave by the resurrection of Christ from the
dead.

Christians' holy rest, therefore, on the first day of the
week, keeps the testimony of the one living and true God,
assured by the resurrection, his Messiaship proven by the resurrection.   The first day of the week, on which Jesus rose, was
devoted to instructing the disciples in the things of his kingdom. to expounding the scriptures and worship, with the

evening spent in the presence of the risen Savior; see Luke 24th chapter, John 20th chapter and Matthew 28th chapter. Jesus then withdrew his visable presence from the disciples for the next six days, and met with them on the next. "And after eight days again his disciples were within, then came Jesus and stood in the midst;" see John 20—26. Both holy days are here counted, as in the feast of tabernacles, Leviticus 23—39. Six consecutive days in which "work may be done," preceeded and followed by a holy day, making the number eight. Commencing the new covenant and the new covenant week with a holy day, by which he established the new covenant week on the divine order of the first covenant week, six days of work followed by a holy rest; without which holy rest, trade and traffic, see John 2—14 and 15, would intrude to the exclusion of spiritual worship in the house of God.

"There remaineth therefore a rest to the people of God;" Hebrews 4—9. As under the first covenant, holy rest like a flaming sword, guarded the commemoration of divine testimony, so also under the new covenant holy rest *remains* to guard the commemoration of the divine Savior. "This do in remembrance of me;" Luke 22—19.

The practice of the apostolic church was in accordance with the foregoing views; see Acts 20—7. Paul was on his way to Jerusalem and in haste, "for he hasted if it were possible for him to be at Jerusalem on the day of pentecost; verse 16. Notwithstanding he abode at Troas seven days to enjoy a Christian Sabbath and communion service with the disciples. While Paul tarried, the seventh day of the Jewish week came and went, unobserved and unnoticed by the disciples. "And upon the first day of the week when the disciples came together to break bread, Paul preached unto them, ready to depart on the morrow, and continued his speech until midnight;" Acts 20—7. "Even till break of day, so he departed;" verse 11.

Some have misled themselves and others by claiming that the first day of the week commenced at *evening* and that the preaching of Paul also commenced at that time and continued to break of day and that then Paul went on his journey.

This hypothesis makes Saint Paul to resume his journey at the break of day on the morning of the first day of the week; the object being to make an artificial apostolic example and by that to prove that Saint Paul regarded the first day of the week *not* as a holy day unto the Lord, but as a day of survile labors, of business and travel.

It will be exceeding liberal to admit that this error has a shadow of justification, and only the poor one of going back upon some of the first covenant holy days "which is abolished," See Leviticus 23—32, "From even unto even shall ye celebrate your Sabbath."

But the resurrection day, the first day of the week, the Christian Sabbath, was another day spoken of afterward; Hebrews 4—8. Mapped out in all the gospels, commencing, not at evening, but very early in the morning; "as it began to dawn towards the first day of the week;" see Matthew 28—1, Mark 17—1 and 2, Luke 24—1 and John 20—1.

This new covenant memorial day, limited to Jesus and the resurrection, had its early morning and its succeeding hours of the day in which the risen Savior expounded the Scriptures to two disciples as they walked in the way to Emeas; also the day was closed by the evening of the same day, in which the two disciples returned to Jerusalem and joined in the evening worship, and to be further instructed by Jesus in the new covenant dispensation, with no change in the order of time since the resurrection.

CHAPTER VI.

THE CHRISTIAN'S HOLY DAY; ITS DUTIES AND OBJECT.

The duties of the holy day is resolved into the love of God and our neighbor. This consummation was in view in the primary working of miralces and the appointment of Sabbath days. This will appear by the directions of Christ to the young man, omitting from the decalogue the Sabbath commandment in the law, and supplying its place with the new commandment, "Thou shalt love thy neighbor as thyself;" Matthew 19—16 to 21. See also Romans 13—8 to 10. To know God in an accepted sense, implies and includes the love of God and our neighbor. "Did not thy father eat and drink and do judgement and justice, and then it was well with him? he judged the cause of the poor and needly; then it was well with him; was not this to know me, saith the Lord?"—Jeremiah 22—13 to 19. The great convival Sabbath feasts of the first covenant gathered into their festive assemblies the widow, the fatherless, the stranger, and them for whom nothing is prepared." See Sabbath of weeks, Deuteronomy 16—11, and feast of tabernacles verse 13 to 15; "and thou shalt rejoice in thy feast, thou and thy son and thy daughter and thy man servant and thy maid servant and the Levite, the stranger and the father ess and the widow that are within thy gates."

And the Levites that taught the people said unto all the people "This day is holy unto the Lord your God; go your way, eat the fat and drink the sweet and send portions unto them for whom nothing is prepared; for this day is holy unto our Lord. See Nehemiah 8—9 to 12.

The truth taught by miracles was perpetuated by Sabbath days for the reformation of the world.

This holy day custom of sending portions to them for whom nothing is prepared was a stated practical confession that the earth is the Lord's, agreeing with the original design of those miracles, "That thou mayest know how that the earth is the Lord's;" Exodus 9—29. Idolatry in the form of graven and molten images, in process of time fell into disrepute by the tests to which they were subjected, by the force and divine power of miracles, and again appeared in the love of wealth and position, set up in men's hearts to be finally overcome and destroyed by the new commandment, "thou shalt love thy neighbor as thyself," written in the hear:; "written not with ink but with the spirit of the living God; not in tables of stone but in fleshly tables of the heart;" second Corintians 3—3. Wherefore the ultimate and final overthrow of idolatry is assured by the new commandment, by a divine promise; "For they shall all know me;" Jeremiah 31—31 to 34. A new commandment I give unto you, that ye love one another; as I have loved you, that ye also love one another; John 13—34·

" Then one of them which was a lawyer asked him a question, saying 'Master, which is the great commandment in the law;' Jesus aid unto him, 'Thou shalt love the Lord thy God with all thy heart, and with all thy soul, and with all thy mind; this is the first and great commandment, and the second is like unto it; thou shalt love thy neighbor as thyself.'"

"On these two commandments hang all the law and the prophets;" Matthew 22—35 to 40. "For all the law is fulfilled in one word, even in this, thou shalt love thy neighbor as thyself;" Galatians 5—14. "For this thou shalt not commit adultery, thou shalt not kill, thou shalt not steal, thou shalt not bear false witness, thou shalt not covet;" and if there be any other commandment it is briefly comprehended in this saying, namely, "thou shalt love thy neighbor as thyself;" Romans 13—9. St. Paul here shows a supplementary commandment which fulfills every law and commandment the decalogue written on tables of stone, namely, "thou shalt love thy neighbor as thyself. "Love worketh no ill to his neighbor therefore love is the fulfilling of the law;" verse 10. The apostolic churches were planted and watered and grew to maturity in love and harmony with the practice of the holy day duties; "Praying us with much entreaty that we would receive the gift and take upon us the fellowship of the ministering to the saints;" second Corinthians 8—4. See also First Corinthians 16—1 and 2. "Now concerning the collection for the saints, as I have given order to the churches of Galatia, even so do ye. Upon the first day of the week let every one of you lay by him in store as God hath prospered him."